An Old Fashioned Love Song

Wise Publications
London/New York/Sydney

8.95

Exclusive Distributors:
Music Sales Limited
8/9 Frith Street,
London W1V 5TZ, England.
Music Sales Pty Limited
120 Rothschild Avenue,
Rosebery, NSW 2018,
Australia.

This book © Copyright 1991 by Wise Publications
Order No.AM85382
ISBN 0-7119-2716-2

Cover and book design by Pearce Marchbank Studio
Compiled by Peter Evans

Music Sales' complete catalogue lists thousands of titles and is
free from your local music shop, or direct from Music Sales Limited.
Please send a cheque/postal order for £1.50 for postage to:
Music Sales Limited, Newmarket Road, Bury St. Edmunds, Suffolk IP33 3YB.

Your Guarantee of Quality

As publishers, we strive to produce every book to the
highest commercial standards.
The book has been carefully designed to minimise awkward
page turns and to make playing from it a real pleasure.
Particular care has been given to specifying acid-free,
neutral-sized paper which has not been chlorine bleached
but produced with special regard for the environment.
Throughout, the printing and binding have been planned
to ensure a sturdy, attractive publication which
should give years of enjoyment.
If your copy fails to meet our high standards, please
inform us and we will gladly replace it.

Printed in the United Kingdom by
Dotesios Limited, Trowbridge, Wiltshire.

An Old Fashioned Love Song

Words & Music by Paul Williams

nev-er go.—

You'll swear you've heard it be-fore— as it slow-ly ram-bles on and on.—

No need in bring-ing 'em back—'cause they've nev-er real-ly gone.

Just An Old —— Fash-ioned love —— Song, ——————

Honkey-tonk style

To Coda ⊕

5

com-ing down___ in three part har - mo-ny.___

Just An Old ___ Fash-ioned Love ___ Song, _____

One I'm sure___ they wrote ___ for you and me, to weave our dreams up-on ___ and

lis-ten to ___ each eve-ning when the lights ___ are low. ___

7

And I Love You So

Words & Music by Don McLean

1.-3. And I love you so,
2. And you love me too,

The peo - ple ask me how.
Your thoughts are just for me,

How I've lived till now,
You set my spir - it free,

I tell them I don't know.
I'm hap - py that you do.

I guess they un - der - stand,
The book of life is brief,

The Lorelei

Music by Barclay Allen. Words by Jerry Gladstone & Rosetta Bent

14

Put Your Head On My Shoulder

Words & Music by Paul Anka

Put your head on my should-er, Hold me in your arms, Ba-by.

Squeeze me oh so tight, Show me That you love me too._____

_____ Put your lips close to mine, dear. Won't you kiss me once, Ba-by?

These Foolish Things

Words by Eric Maschwitz. Music by Jack Strachey

REFRAIN

1. A ci-gar-ette that bears a lip-stick's tra-ces........
2. Gar-den-ia per-fume ling-'ring on a pil-low........
3. First daf-fo-dils and long ex-ci-ted ca-bles........

D   Em9 C(susF#) A9

An air-line tick-et to ro-man-tic pla-ces........
Wild straw-b'ries on-ly se-ven francs a ki-lo..........
And can-dle-light on lit-tle cor-ner ta-bles......

D   Bm7   Em9   E9/A   A+7

And still my heart has wings........ These fool-ish
And still my heart has wings........ These fool-ish
And still my heart has wings........ These fool-ish

D9   D+7   G6   B9

things   Re-mind me of you.
things   Re-mind me of you.
things   Re-mind me of you.

Em9   E9   A11   E+7   A9

20

A tink - ling pi - a - no in the next a - part - ment,....
The Park at ev - 'ning when the bell has sound - ed..........
The smile of Gar - bo and the scent of ro - ses,........

D   Bm7   Gmaj7   C(susF#)   A9

Those stumb - ling words that told you what my heart meant,
The "Ile de France" with all the gulls a - round it.........
The wait - ers whist - ling as the last bar clo - ses

D   Bm   E9   A7   A+7

A fair - ground's paint - ed swings........ These fool - ish
The beau - ty that is spring's,.... These fool - ish
The song that Cros - by sings_____ These fool - ish

D9   D+7   G6   Am6/B   B7(9b)

things Re - mind me of you.
things Re - mind me of you.
things Re - mind me of you.

E9   A7   D

21

A te - le - phone that rings__ but who's to ans - wer?......
Silk stock - ings thrown a - side, dance in - vi - ta - tions......
Two lo - vers on the street who walk like dream - ers.........

D   Bm7   Em9 E9 A9

Oh, how the ghost of you clings!   These fool - ish
Oh, how the ghost of you clings!   These fool - ish
Oh, how the ghost of you clings!   These fool - ish

poco cresc.

D9   D13 D+7 D7   Gmaj7   E9

things............ Re-mind me of you.   you.
things............ Re-mind me of you.   you.
things.. .... Re-mind me of you.   you.

D6   A+7(9♭)   D6   C9   A+7 D6

You're Nobody 'Til Somebody Loves You

Words & Music by Russ Morgan, Larry Stock & James Cavanaugh

Verse

Some look for glo-ry, It's still the old sto-ry Of love ver-sus glo-ry, And when all is said and done, _____

It's Impossible (Somos Novios)

Words by Sid Wayne. Music by A. Manzanero

arr. by Frank Metis

Because Of You

Words & Music by Arthur Hammerstein & Dudley Wilkinson

All my days were lone-ly ones, till you came a-long. Now my days are hap-py ones; you filled my life with song.

CHORUS

Be - cause of you there's a song in my

Memories Are Made Of This

Words & Music by Terry Gilkyson, Richard Dehr & Frank Miller

Don't for - get a small moon - beam
With some bless - ings from a - bove

Fold in light - ly with a dream.
Serve it gen - 'rous - ly with love.

Your lips and mine, Two sips of wine, Mem - or -
One man, one wife, One love thro' life, Mem - or -

ies are made of this.
ies are made of this.

To Coda ⊕

Then add the

34

This Guy's In Love With You

Words by Hal David. Music by Burt Bacharach

Moderately slow, with a light beat

You see___ this guy, ___ this guy's in love with you.___

___ Yes, I'm___ in love.___ Who

There I've Said It Again

Words & Music by Redd Evans & Dave Mann

phrase that would sum up all that I feel for you. But what good are phras-es? The

thought that a-maz-es is you love me,— and it's hea-ven-ly. For-give me__ for

want-ing you so,— but one thing__ I want you to know, I've loved you since

hea-ven knows when.__ There! I've said it a-gain.__ I've

When You're In Love With A Beautiful Woman

Words & Music by Even Stevens

As Time Goes By

Words & Music by Herman Hupfeld

Moderato, con espressione

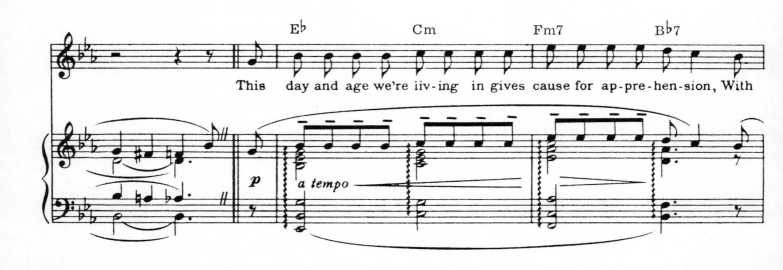

This day and age we're liv-ing in gives cause for ap-pre-hen-sion, With

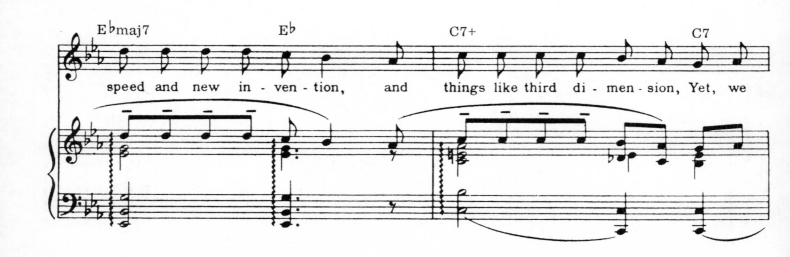

speed and new in-ven-tion, and things like third di-men-sion, Yet, we

Try A Little Tenderness

Words & Music by Harry Woods, Jimmy Campbell & Reg Connelly

wo - man loves a man, _____ He's a he - ro in her
wor - ries drag you down, _____ It's so ea - sy to for -

eyes, _____ And a he - ro he can al - ways be, If
get. _____ But make the ef - fort just the same, And

he'll just re - al - ize.
see the thrill you'll get.

CHORUS Tenderly

She may be wea - ry,

Wo - men do get wea - ry, Wear - ing the same shab - by dress,

And when she's wea-ry, Try a lit-tle ten-der - ness.

You know she's wait-ing, Just an-ti-ci-pat-ing, Things she may nev-er poss-

ess. While she's with-out them, Try a lit-tle ten-der - ness.

It's not just sen-ti-men-tal,_____ She

More Than I Can Say

Words & Music by Sonny Curtis & Jerry Allison

I'm Gettin' Sentimental Over You

Words by Ned Washington. Music by Geo. Bassman

Love's Roundabout (La Ronde De L'Amour)

French Words by Louis Ducreux. English Words by Harold Purce. Music by Oscar Straus

note float on the blue; While the fair - ground
mon - te en tour - noy - ant. El - le quit - te

tune is ring - ing, Back the thrill will still come
no - tre ter - re, No - tre ter - re noire et

D.%. al Coda

wing - ing, You will have me, And I shall have you.
clai - re Qui tourne et dan - se d'un même é - lan.

CODA

round - a - bout.
de l'a - mour!

accel.

ff

63

The Very Thought Of You

Words & Music by Ray Noble

I don't need your pho-to-graph, To keep by my bed;
I hold you re-spon-si-ble, I'll take it to law,

Your pic - ture is al -ways in my head.
I nev - er have felt like this be - fore.

I don't need your por-trait, dear, To call you to mind,
I'm su - ing for dam-ag - es, Ex-cus - es won't do,

(I Love You) For Sentimental Reasons

Words & Music by Derek Watson & William Best

This Is My Song

Words & Music by Charles Chaplin

Barcarolle

Why is my heart so light?

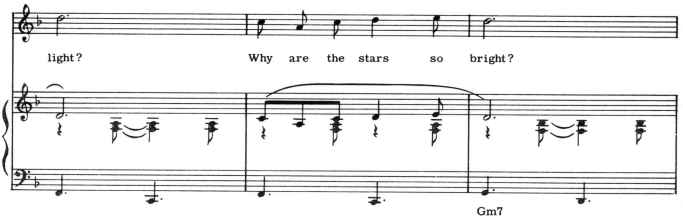

Why are the stars so bright?

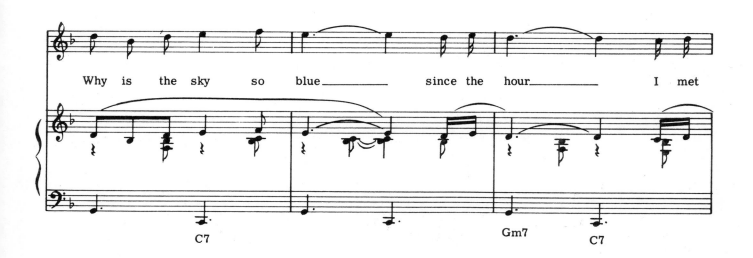

Why is the sky so blue_____ since the hour_____ I met

you?_____ A - lone I sing in moon-light_____ with

you in my heart su - preme_____ To hear you say "I

love____ you"_____ That is my hope, my dream.

Rubato

Love,_____ this is my song,_____ Here is a song,___ a ser-en-ade to

you_____ The world_____ cannot be wrong_____ If in this world_____ there's

you. _____ I care not what the world may say_____ with-out your love there is no

day._____ Love, _____ this is my song, _____ Here is a song a serenade to_____

you.

you.

Unchained Melody

Music by Alex North. Words by Hy Zaret

Can't Help Lovin' Dat Man

Music by Jerome Kern. Words by Oscar Hammerstein II

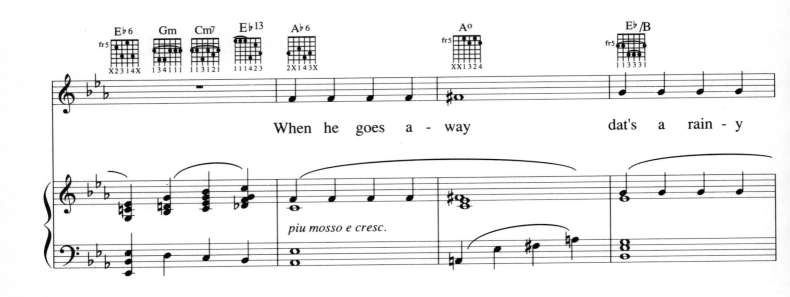

When he goes a - way   dat's a rain - y

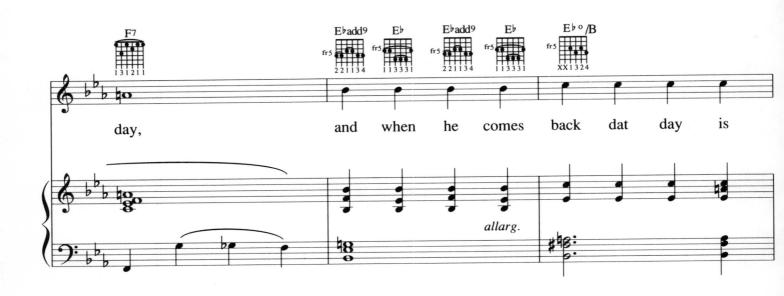

day,   and when he comes back dat day is

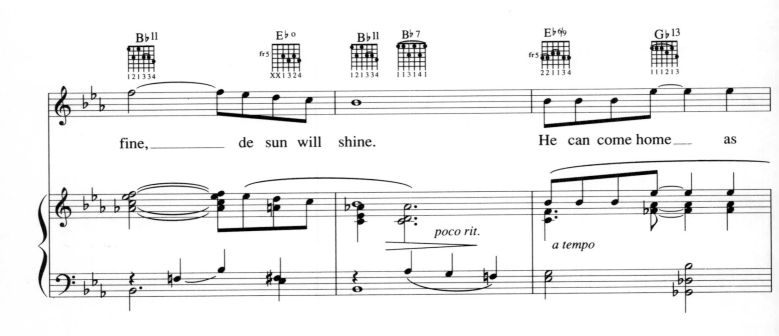

fine,_____ de sun will shine.   He can come home___ as

late as can be,___ home wid-out him___ ain't no home to me,___

Can't help lov-in' dat man___ of mine.

1.

2.

mine.___

rall.

They Didn't Believe Me

Music by Jerome Kern. Words by Herbert Reynolds

Slowly, with expression

All The Things You Are

Music by Jerome Kern. Words by Oscar Hammerstein II

Moderately, with expression

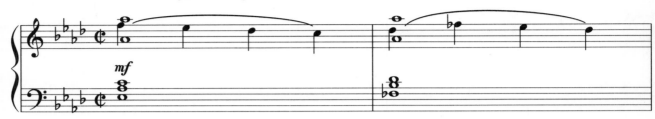

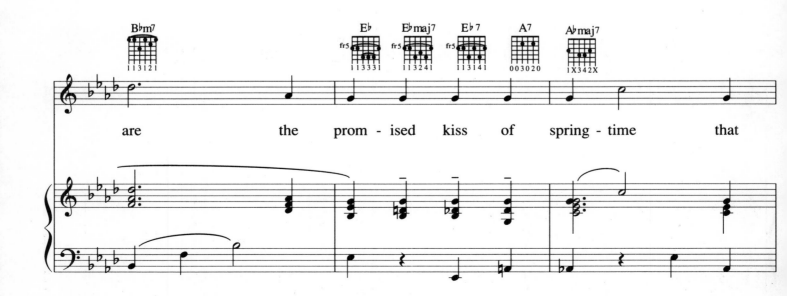

makes the lone - ly win - ter seem long.

You are the

breath - less hush of eve - ning that trem - bles on the

brink of a love - ly song._____ You are the

ang - el glow____ that lights a star,_____

____ the dear - est things I know____ are what you

Moonglow

Words & Music by Will Hudson, Eddie de Lange & Irving Mills

Somewhere

Music by Leonard Bernstein. Lyrics by Stephen Sondheim

Slowly

There's a place for us, Some-where a place for us.

Peace and quiet_ and op - en air wait for us some - where._

Strangers In The Night

Words by Charles Singleton & Eddie Snyder. Music by Bert Kaempfert

Moderately slow

Stran- gers in the night _____ ex- chang-ing glanc- es, won- d'ring in the night _____ what were the chanc- es we'd be shar-ing love _____ be- fore the night was through. _____ Some-thing in your eyes _____ was so in-vit- ing,

September Morn

Words & Music by Neil Diamond & Gilbert Becaud

Moderately slow

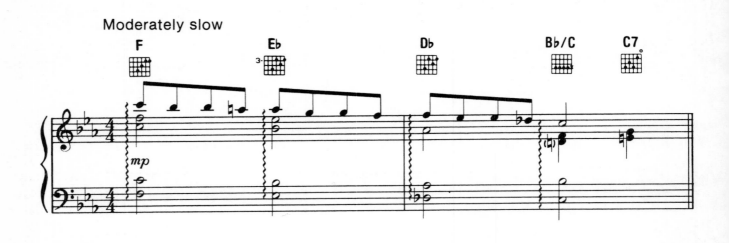

Stay for just a while. Stay and let me look at you.

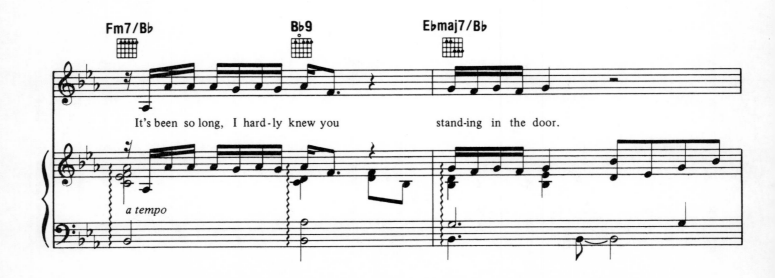

It's been so long, I hard-ly knew you standing in the door.

Moments To Remember

Words & Music by Robert Allen & Al Stillman

On A Slow Boat To China

Words & Music by Frank Loesser

Slowly, with a beat

I'd love to get you____ On A Slow Boat To Chi-na,____
All to my-self,____ a - lone.____
Get you and keep you____ in my arms ev - er - more,____

Till Then

Words & Music by Guy Wood, Eddie Seller & Sol Marcus

Slowly, with expression

The Twelfth Of Never

Words by Paul Francis Webster. Music by Jerry Livingston

Very slowly, with feeling

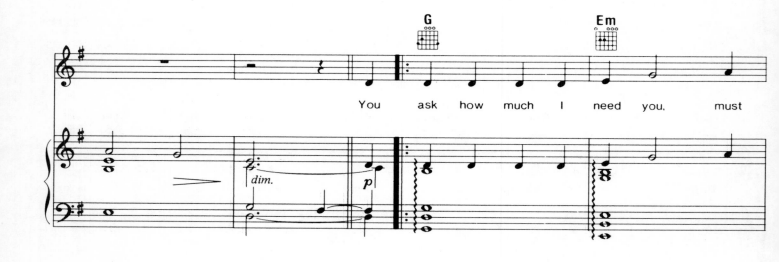

You ask how much I need you, must

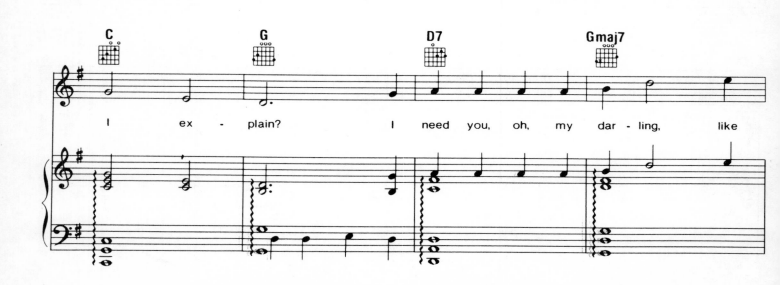

I ex - plain? I need you, oh, my dar - ling, like

rhyme, Until the Twelfth of Nev - er, And

that's a long, long time; Un - til the Twelfth of

Nev - er; And that's a long, long time. You

that's a long, long time.

I've Got You Under My Skin

Words & Music by Cole Porter

Love Will Keep Us Together

Music by Neil Sedaka. Words by Howard Greenfield

If You Leave Me Now

Words & Music by Peter Cetera

128